Would you prefer to walk or drive a buggy on the Moon?

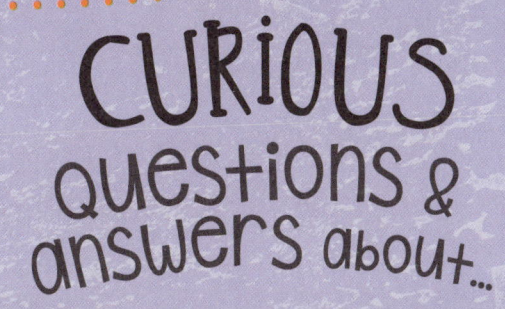

CURIOUS Questions & answers about...

Space Machines

What experiments would you like to do in space?

Who would you take with you on a trip to the International Space Station?

Would you rather orbit the Moon or Mars?

Words by Anne Rooney
Illustrations by Lucy Semple

Miles Kelly

What are space machines?

Any machines that are sent into space! They include rockets, shuttles, satellites and probes.

I travel around (orbit) Earth and keep track of the weather.

Meteosat weather satellite

Hubble Space Telescope

Falcon 9 rocket

I look far into space and take photos.

Space starts 80–100 kilometres above Earth's sea level.

"I blast spacecraft from Earth into space."

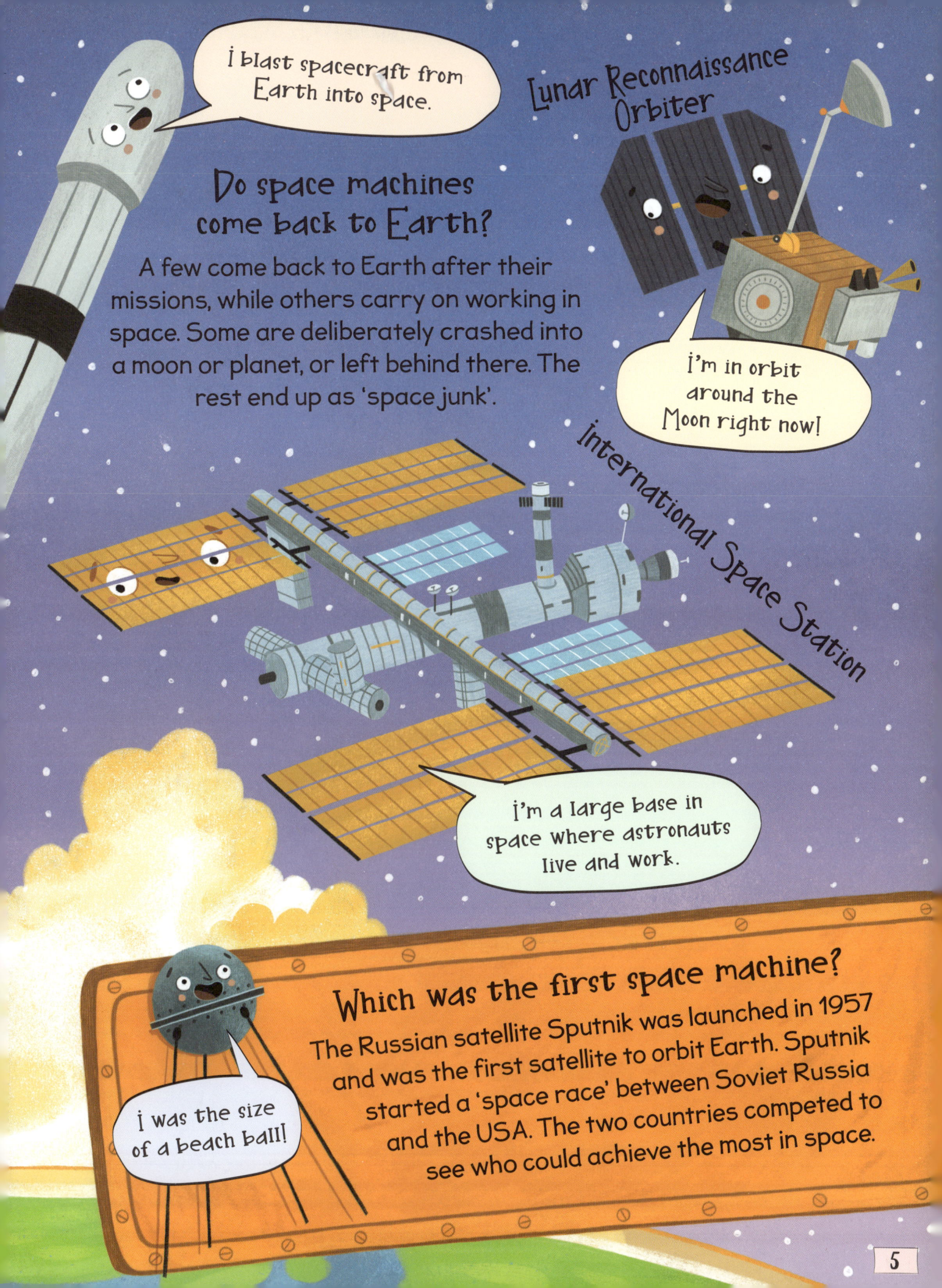

Do space machines come back to Earth?

A few come back to Earth after their missions, while others carry on working in space. Some are deliberately crashed into a moon or planet, or left behind there. The rest end up as 'space junk'.

Lunar Reconnaissance Orbiter

"I'm in orbit around the Moon right now!"

International Space Station

"I'm a large base in space where astronauts live and work."

Which was the first space machine?

The Russian satellite Sputnik was launched in 1957 and was the first satellite to orbit Earth. Sputnik started a 'space race' between Soviet Russia and the USA. The two countries competed to see who could achieve the most in space.

"I was the size of a beach ball!"

5

Which was the biggest rocket?

The Saturn V rockets used to carry the Apollo spacecraft to the Moon were the largest rockets that have ever launched.

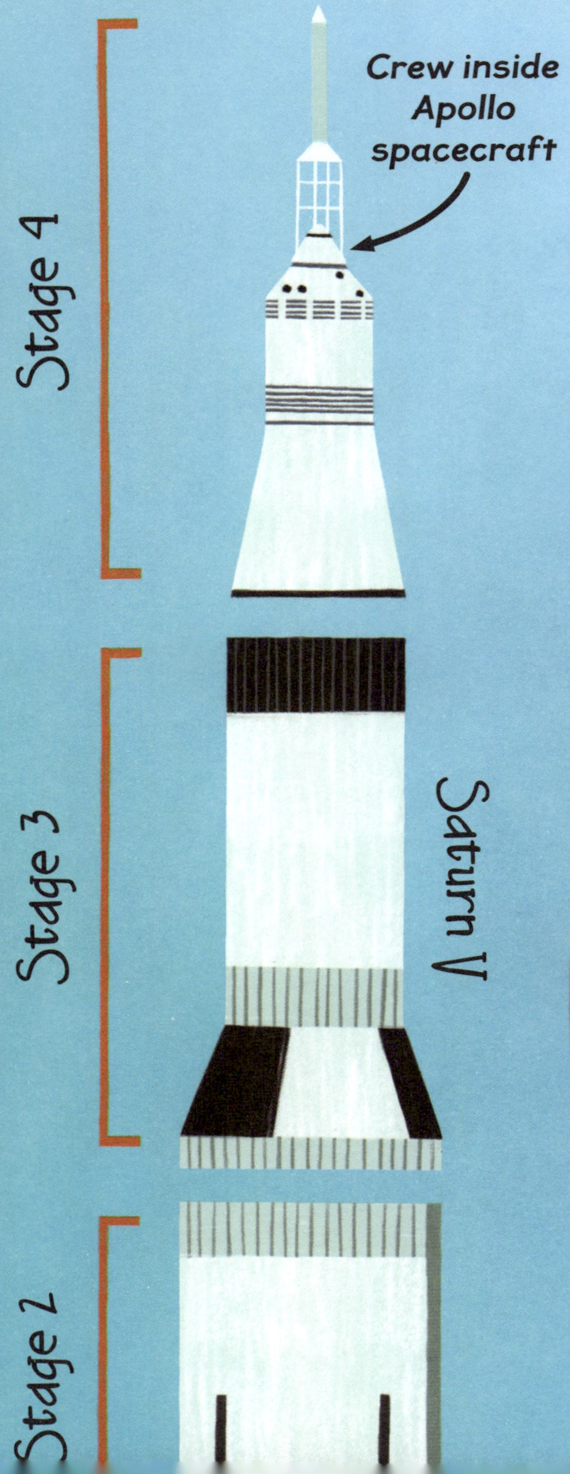

How do rockets take off?

At launch, rockets stand upright. They burn huge amounts of liquid or solid fuel, which makes a lot of exhaust. This blasts out of the back of the rocket, pushing it upwards.

Crew inside Apollo spacecraft

Saturn V

Stage 4

Stage 3

Stage 2

Stage 3 falls away

Stage 4 goes off on its own!

Stage 3 fires twice – once to place the craft in orbit and again to send it towards its destination.

Stage 2 falls away

As well as using fuel, spacecraft can swing past a planet or moon, using its gravity to change their speed and direction.

Why do rockets come apart?

Each stage of a rocket contains a store of fuel and oxygen. When this is burnt up in the engines, the stage comes apart and falls away. When the stage has been used, it is no longer useful.

USA

Stage 1

Stage 1 falls away

Earth

Stage 2 puts it near its orbit above Earth.

Stage 1 launches the rocket.

7

Who was the first person in space?

In 1961, Russian Yuri Gagarin travelled into space in Vostok 1 – a tiny capsule launched by a rocket. It circled Earth once, taking 89 minutes, then came back down. Gagarin left the craft with a parachute.

Cosmonaut Yuri Gagarin.

No people travelled in Luna 2.

Which spacecraft landed on the Moon first?

The Russian Luna 2 in 1959. Lots of spacecraft have been to the Moon since then, including six American Apollo craft carrying astronauts.

How did Apollo land on the Moon?

After being launched by a Saturn V rocket, the Apollo spacecraft was pulled into orbit by the Moon's gravity. A lander then separated and went down to the Moon's surface.

The service and command module stayed in space.

Who was first to walk on the Moon?

"Me! I'm an American astronaut called Neil Armstrong."

"And I was next. I'm Buzz Aldrin. We went together on Apollo 11 in 1969."

"I'm Michael Collins. I stayed in the command module."

When the astronauts were ready to leave the Moon, thrusters blasted part of the lander back up into space to rejoin the service and command module.

"This is much easier than walking!"

The Moon buggy could drive over objects up to 30 centimetres high.

Did the astronauts have a car on the Moon?

Kind of! The last three Apollo missions in 1971 and 1972 took a Moon buggy to drive on the surface.

9

How many?

2.5 million
The number of parts in a space shuttle.

40,300
The speed in kilometres per hour a rocket needs to reach to leave Earth's atmosphere.

5 space shuttles were built and flew into space many times. There were **135** flights.

There are **8** layers in the Extravehicular Mobility Unit worn for spacewalks.

1 million
The number of people the technology company SpaceX hope to have living on Mars in 100 years.

1323
The total number of flight-days of the five NASA space shuttles over 30 years.

924,675
The number of litres of fuel used by the first stage of a Saturn V rocket.

10 space stations have successfully launched and been occupied.

0.14 The top speed in kilometres per hour of the Curiosity Mars rover.

18 The top speed in kilometres per hour of the Moon buggy.

There are **128 million** pieces of space junk one millimetre to one centimetre wide orbiting Earth right now.

Only **1** space station is still operational.

How are satellites placed in space?

Rockets and space shuttles have carried satellites into space. A rocket carries the satellite to the right height, then fires smaller rockets to adjust its position and release the satellite.

The Moon

I'm Earth's only natural satellite!

Why don't they float off into space?

Satellites are held in place by Earth's gravity. They use thrusters to stay up as they start to slip towards Earth over time.

What are they used for?

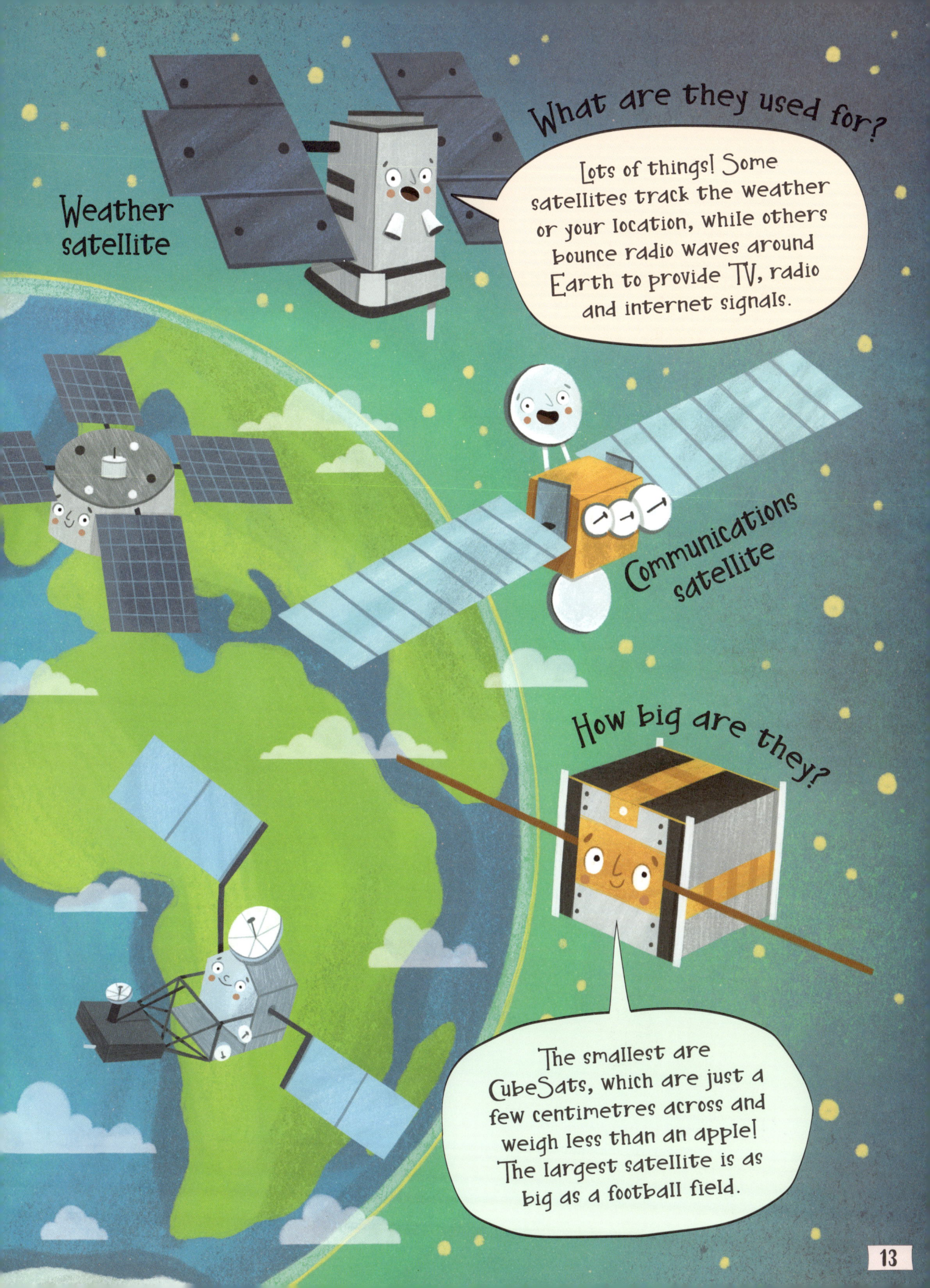

Weather satellite

Lots of things! Some satellites track the weather or your location, while others bounce radio waves around Earth to provide TV, radio and internet signals.

Communications satellite

How big are they?

The smallest are CubeSats, which are just a few centimetres across and weigh less than an apple! The largest satellite is as big as a football field.

Would you rather?

Be the **first** human on **Mars**...

...or **first** to find a desert **island**?

Would you rather **discover** a new **planet** with a telescope...

...or **visit** the Moon?

What's better? A **holiday** on the International Space Station or **climbing** Mount Everest?

Would you prefer to invent a **spaceship** that could travel to Jupiter in one day...

...or a **flying car**?

Would you rather have a **rocket** or a **satellite** named after you?

...or your favourite **movie star**?

Who would you like to **meet** more, an **alien**...

Would you prefer to spend a day in **zero gravity**...

...or seeing **great white sharks** in the wild?

What's better? Going on a **spacewalk** or controlling the **space station**?

15

What is the International Space Station?

It's a research base in space. Built from modules arranged along a solid metal backbone, it is powered by solar panels. Astronauts live there for six months at a time.

Robotic arm

Solar panels

How was it built?
The ISS was built in space, from modules carried up separately by rockets and in the space shuttle. A robotic arm and astronauts bolted all the parts together.

How do astronauts get to the ISS?

At first they were carried by a space shuttle, which went to the ISS and came back to Earth. Now they go in a Russian Soyuz craft and return in its descent module.

International Space Station (ISS)

Space shuttle

Is the ISS speedy?

Yes! The ISS travels at 8 kilometres per second at a height of 360 kilometres. It covers a distance equivalent to the Moon and back every day!

What's life like on board?

It's not easy! There is zero gravity, so the crew float about. This makes eating, drinking, washing and going to the toilet more difficult!

Every day is a bad hair day in space!

17

What is an EMU?

The EMU (Extravehicular Mobility Unit) is like a mini spacecraft worn by astronauts. It allows them to go on spacewalks outside their spacecraft. The EMU has a life support system and a jetpack.

Helmet with camera

Hard upper torso

Lights

> My EMU backpack provides air, and keeps me at the right temperature and pressure.

Primary life support system

Arms

Control module with displays

Tether

Why do astronauts go on spacewalks?

Astronauts go on spacewalks to fix or change parts of the ISS, or to mend satellites. They also place or check experiments on the outside of the ISS that test the effects of space on objects or processes.

Why don't astronauts float away?

Astronauts attach their tether to different parts of the spacecraft so they stay tethered as they move. They can also use the rescue module of their EMU backpack, which has 24 jet thrusters to move them around.

Robotic arm

I am ready to move astronauts around the ISS and catch spacecraft.

Checklist

Gloves

Lower torso assembly

What is the robotic arm used for?

The ISS has a hinged 'arm' with a 'hand' at each end. One end grabs onto the space station while the other end carries astronauts, moves equipment and secures docking spacecraft.

Boots

19

Saturn

What are space probes?

Probes are unmanned robotic spacecraft. They go on long journeys to explore objects in space, including planets, moons, asteroids and comets. Some probes carry landers, which they release onto the surface of a planet or other object.

How are probes controlled?

By computer. Some of a probe's activities are programmed in advance while others are controlled from Earth. When a probe is far away it can take hours for radio signals to reach it, so it needs to make some 'decisions' itself.

What do probes do?

We take photos and make measurements, which we send back to Earth by radio link. I'm Cassini! At the end of my work, I plunged into the atmosphere of Saturn, making measurements on the way down!

Huygens

What do landers do?

We take photos and collect information about conditions on the surface and send these back to Earth. I'm Huygens! I separated from Cassini and used parachutes to land on one of Saturn's moons.

Cassini

Titan, one of Saturn's moons

21

Have spacecraft been to Mars?

By 2019, 56 spacecraft had set off for Mars and 26 had been successful. Some are still in orbit around Mars, while some landers are still on the surface.

Sky crane lowering Curiosity

I use thrusters to slow me down, and lower the lander on a strong cable.

How do spacecraft get to Mars?

A rocket launches the craft into space, points it in the right direction and lets go! It takes about 7-8 months to get to Mars and the trip needs careful planning, as both Earth and Mars are moving.

How do landers land?

They use thrusters pointing downwards to slow their fall to the surface. Thrusters push them upwards while gravity pulls them down. The Curiosity rover was lowered by a sky crane!

What can orbiters do?

"Orbiters look down on the whole planet as they travel around it. They measure gases, temperature and the height of the land, and take photos."

Mars Reconnaissance Orbiter

"My top speed is just 140 metres an hour!"

Curiosity

Can rovers look for life on Mars?

Yes! Rovers are landers that can move around, gathering information from different places. They look in close detail at the soil and rock, and can look for chemical signs of life.

Have any spacecraft left the Solar System?

Yes! Two Voyager spacecraft have left our Solar System and are journeying into interstellar space (the space between stars). Voyager 1 has travelled the furthest.

Golden record

Will the Voyagers meet aliens?

Maybe! If they do, each craft has a 'golden record' with information for any intelligent aliens, including sounds and photos of Earth.

Voyager 1

Where is Voyager 1 going?

Just to 'outer space'! In a billion years it could be about halfway across our galaxy. It will keep going until something destroys it, which could be millions, perhaps billions, of years in the future.

I'm around 20 billion kilometres from Earth! I travel at about 60,000 kilometres an hour and can cover half a billion kilometres per year.

Which spacecraft has visited the most distant object?

NASA's New Horizons probe flew close to an asteroid in the Kuiper Belt, called Arrokoth, in 2019. It took 9.5 years to get to Pluto, and another 3.5 years to reach Arrokoth.

New Horizons

Arrokoth

Did you know?

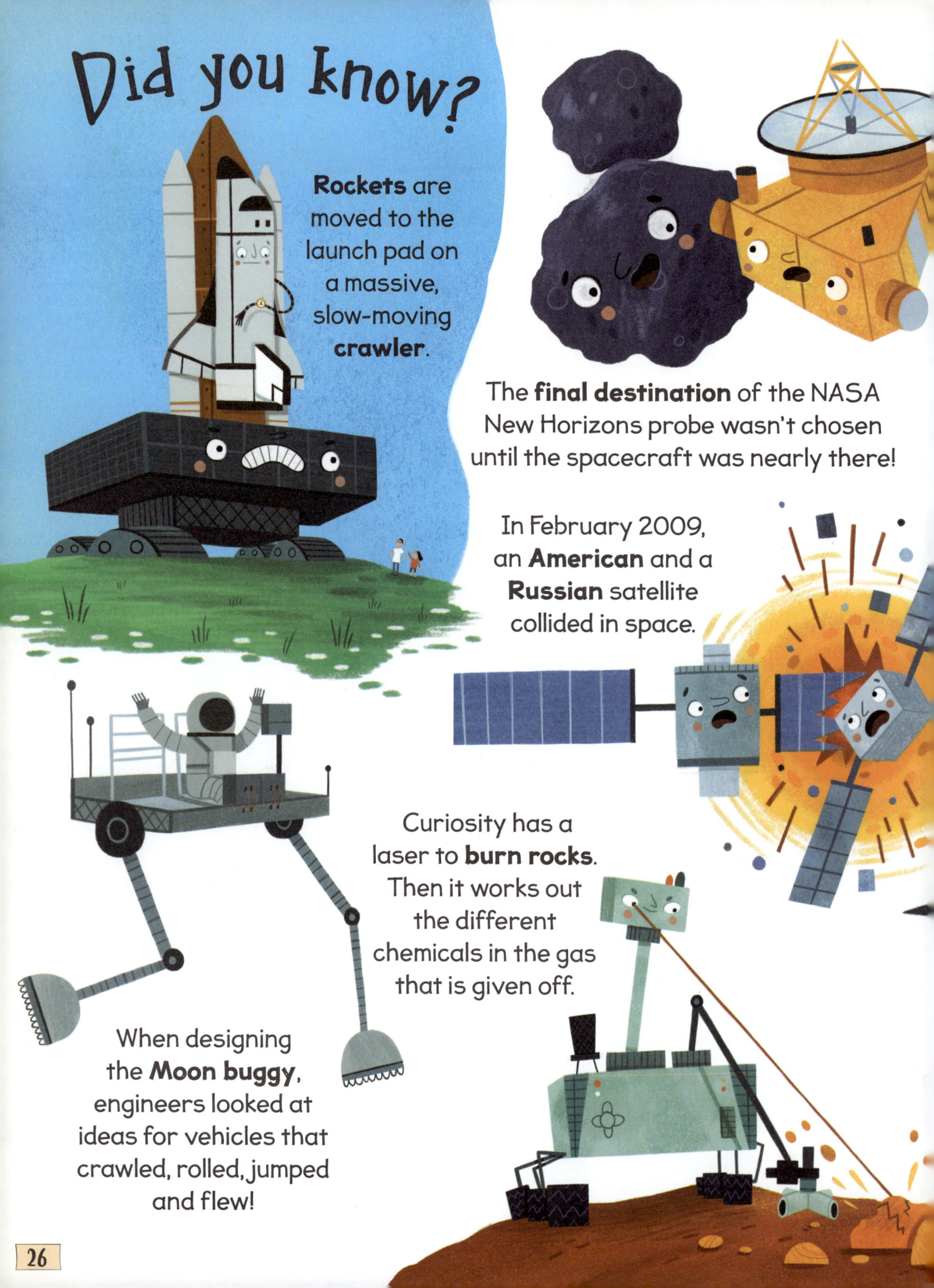

Rockets are moved to the launch pad on a massive, slow-moving **crawler**.

The **final destination** of the NASA New Horizons probe wasn't chosen until the spacecraft was nearly there!

In February 2009, an **American** and a **Russian** satellite collided in space.

Curiosity has a laser to **burn rocks**. Then it works out the different chemicals in the gas that is given off.

When designing the **Moon buggy**, engineers looked at ideas for vehicles that crawled, rolled, jumped and flew!

26

The Japanese spacecraft IKAROS is the first to use a **solar sail**.

The **computer** used to land on the Moon was less powerful than a modern **smart phone**.

Nooooooo!

The probe Cassini **plunged into Saturn** to avoid colliding with any moons.

There is a **Tesla car** in orbit around Earth.

The Chinese Chang'e 4 lander and rover Yutu were the **first to land** on the far side of the Moon, in 2019.

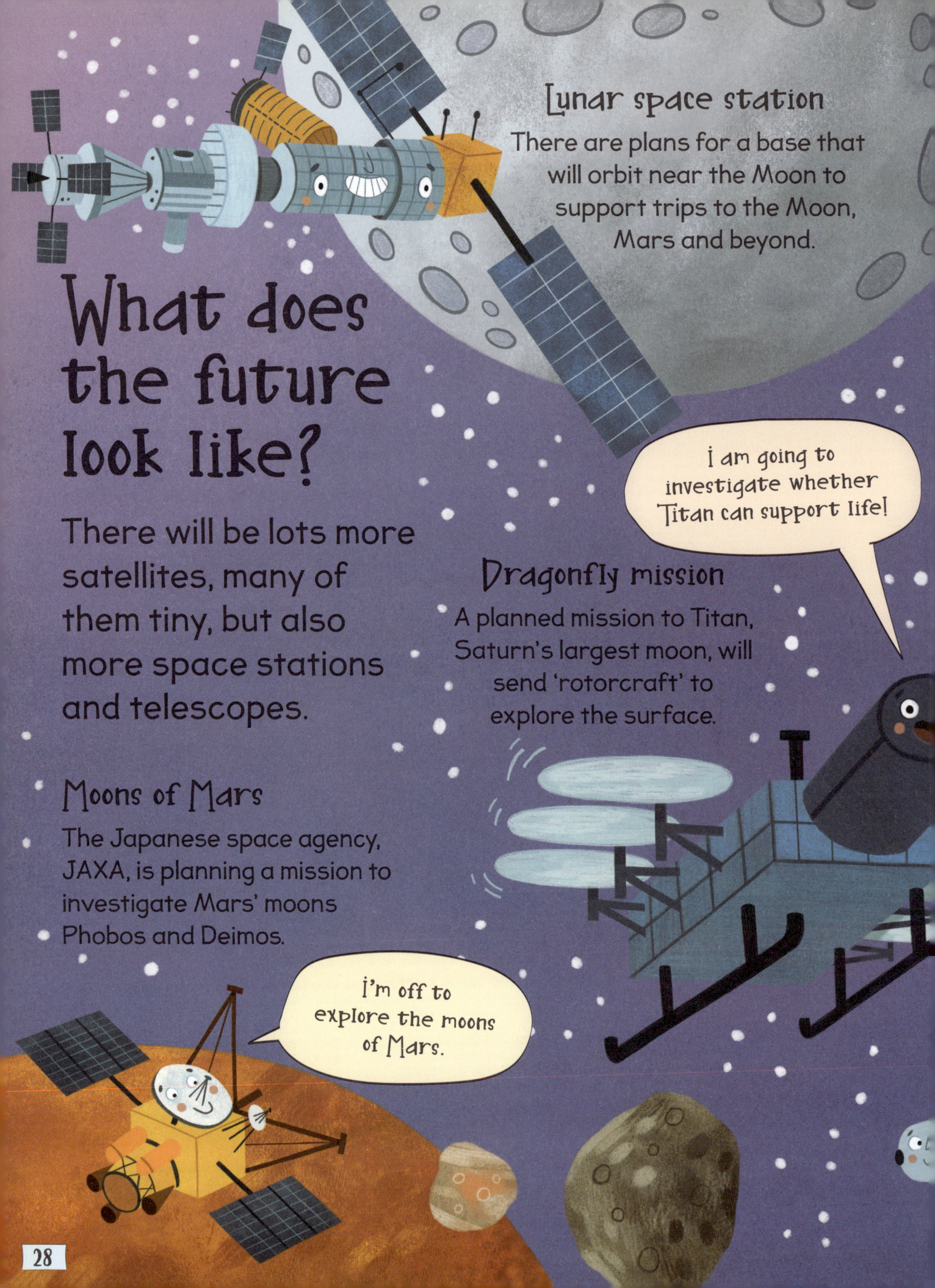

Lunar space station
There are plans for a base that will orbit near the Moon to support trips to the Moon, Mars and beyond.

What does the future look like?

There will be lots more satellites, many of them tiny, but also more space stations and telescopes.

I am going to investigate whether Titan can support life!

Dragonfly mission
A planned mission to Titan, Saturn's largest moon, will send 'rotorcraft' to explore the surface.

Moons of Mars
The Japanese space agency, JAXA, is planning a mission to investigate Mars' moons Phobos and Deimos.

I'm off to explore the moons of Mars.

Mission to Mercury

The BepiColombo probe, launched by JAXA and ESA in 2018, will travel to Mercury, arriving in 2025.

Sail to the stars

We could see new kinds of sails that use solar wind, radiation or even just light to push spacecraft along.

I have been built to launch heavy objects into space!

Asteroid mines

Some organizations are hoping to trap asteroids and mine them for useful metals.

Mega rockets

New types of rocket to launch heavy objects are being developed, including NASA's SLS (super-heavy launch system).

29

A compendium of questions

Do probes ever come back?
The probe itself doesn't, but probes can return capsules. In 2006, the Stardust probe sent back dust from the comet Wild 2.

What does an astronaut wear under their EMU?
A giant nappy, and a body suit that has tubes to carry water and cool their body.

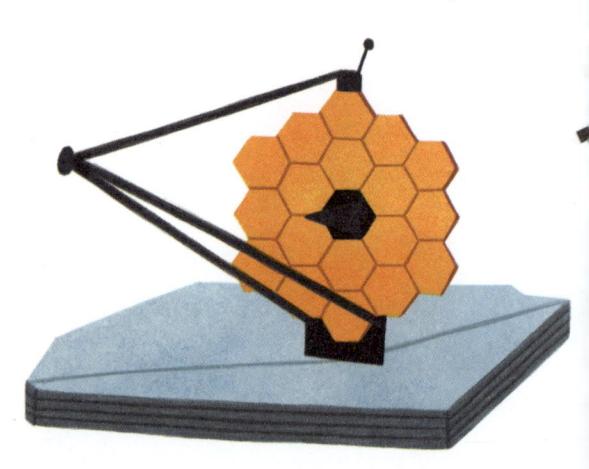

Why have a telescope in space?
It's free from distortion produced by Earth's atmosphere and it can also pick up ultraviolet radiation blocked by Earth's atmosphere.

Are space shuttles still used?
No. The last space shuttle, Endeavour, made its final flight in 2011.

How do astronauts talk to each other in space?
They have a radio link, with microphones in their helmets.

Where are you going?

30